Ladybird Readers

Sunny's Garden

Based on the *My Little Pony* episode
"Ali-Conned"

Picture words

Sunny

Izzy

lo||1

TEN

n

Notes to teachers, parents, and carers

The *Ladybird Readers* Beginner level helps young language learners to become familiar with key conversational phrases in English. The language introduced has clear real-life applications, giving children the tools to hold their first conversations in English.

This book focuses on food and provides practice of saying "can" and "have".

There are some activities to do in this book. They will help children practice these skills:

 Speaking 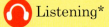 Listening*   Writing   Reading   Singing*

*To complete these activities, listen to the audio downloads available at www.ladybirdeducation.co.uk

Series Editor: Sorrel Pitts
Text adapted by Sorrel Pitts
Song lyrics by Fiona Davis

LADYBIRD BOOKS

UK | USA | Canada | Ireland | Australia
India | New Zealand | South Africa

Ladybird Books is part of the Penguin Random House group of companies
whose addresses can be found at global.penguinrandomhouse.com.
www.penguin.co.uk   www.puffin.co.uk   www.ladybird.co.uk

 Penguin
Random House
UK

Text adapted from *My Little Pony* episode "Ali-Conned" by Hasbro Inc., 2023
This version first published by Ladybird Books, 2023
001

Licensed by:

Printed in China

The authorized representative in the EEA is Penguin Random House Ireland, Morrison Chambers, 32 Nassau Street, Dublin, D02 YH68

A CIP catalogue record for this book is available from the British Library

ISBN: 978–0–241–61695–6

All correspondence to:
Ladybird Books
Penguin Random House Children's
One Embassy Gardens, 8 Viaduct Gardens, London SW11 7BW

FSC
www.fsc.org
MIX
Paper from
responsible sources
FSC® C018179

vegetables

special

Alicorn

"Can we have a garden?"
asks Sunny.

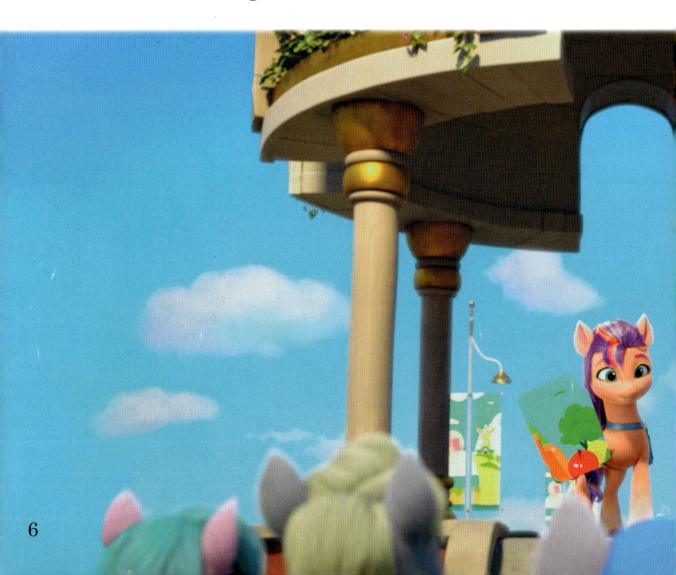

"We can have a lot of fruit
and vegetables."

"No! We do not like fruit and vegetables," say the ponies.

"I can help," says Sunny.
Sunny is now an Alicorn.
She is special.

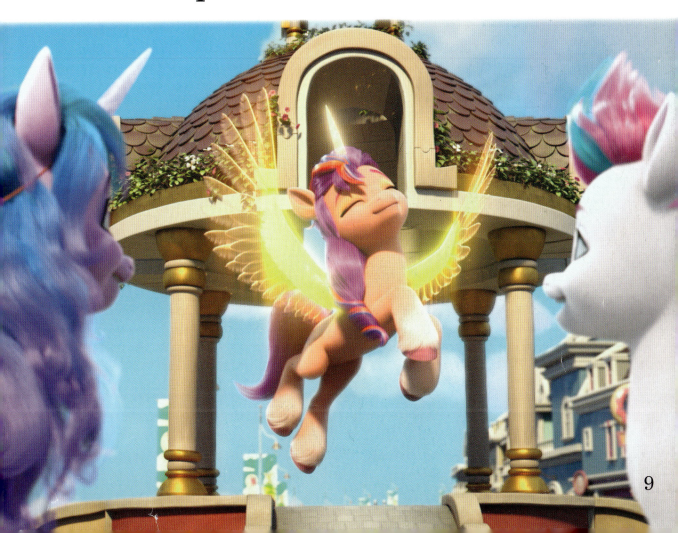

"Look! Sunny is now an Alicorn! She is beautiful. We can help her with her garden," say the ponies.

"I am not special," says Sunny
to Pipp.

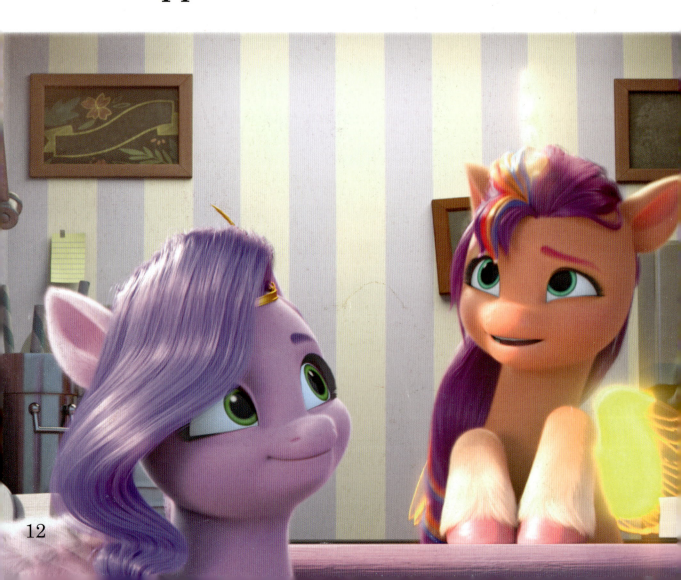

Now, Sunny is sad.

"Do not be sad, Sunny."
says Izzy.

"Come with me," says Izzy.

"Here is your garden!"
say Sunny's friends.

"You are our friend.
You are special to us,"
say the ponies.

"We can eat a lot of fruit and vegetables," says Sunny. "Thank you!"

1 **Talk with a friend.**

Hello!

Hello!

Do you like fruit?

Yes, I do. / No, I do not.

Do you have a garden?

Yes, I do. / No, I do not.

2 Listen. Color in the words. 🎧 📖

1 vegetable   fruit

2 help   see

3 sad   special

4 pony   friend

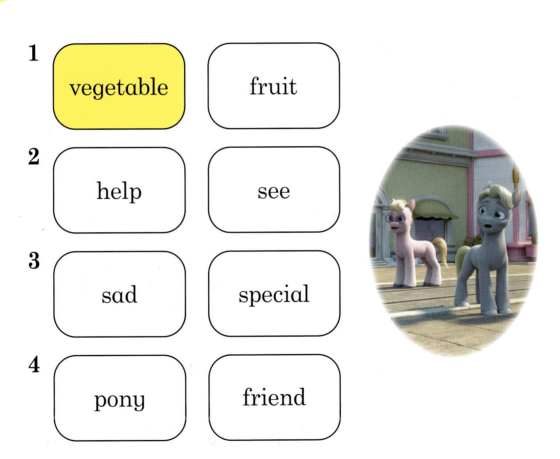

3 Listen. Put a ✓ by the correct words. 🎧 📖

1 **a** "We like fruit
and vegetables." ☐
  b "We do not like fruit
and vegetables." ✓

2 **a** Sunny is sad. ☐
  b Sunny is happy. ☐

3 **a** "Here is your fruit." ☐
  b "Here is your garden." ☐

4 **a** "Come with me." ☐
  b "Thank you!" ☐

4 Listen. Write the first letters. 🎧 ✏️

1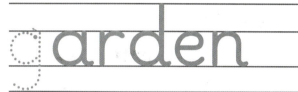

garden

2

vegetables

3

special

5 Sing the song.

Sunny wants a garden.
She loves fruit.
She loves vegetables.
Fruit and vegetables are good for you.

Sunny's friends do not want a garden.
They do not like fruit.
They do not like vegetables.
But Sunny is special. They want to help her.

Then, her friends say, "Here is your garden!
Look at the fruit!
Look at the vegetables!"
Now, Sunny is happy. She says, "Thank you!"